Mommy Motivators

A Collaborative Journal
of Empathy and Support
For New Mothers

Emily Donatelli

ISBN 9781675940747

Cover Illustration by Judy Boyle

Internal artwork icons by Freepik from www.flaticon.com

Printed in USA by KDP

To my little ones, for the joy of being your Mom

Contents

No language can express the
power and beauty and heroism
of a mother's love

Edwin Hubbel Chapin

Preface

A good friend of mine was having a baby and, in preparation for her shower, I went searching through her registry. I picked out a couple items from her list but then decided I wanted to do more. "I want to get her things that **she** will need when she comes home," I told my husband. "I want to get her lanolin, and a sleep mask, and tissues, and water bottles, and...adult diapers!"

I didn't mean to sound silly or crude, but I felt a duty to take care of my friend knowing she would soon be busy taking care of someone else. These are the items I quickly realized that I had a needed after having my own baby. I wanted them well-stocked in every room (or bathroom) of my house!

Other things I wanted to include in this care package were love, a hug, and compassion. Sure, I could plan to visit or call after the baby came but I also knew from having my own baby that visitors and calls can sometimes be overwhelming—especially in the beginning.

I decided to write her five handwritten notes, each sealed in an envelope and labeled appropriately for her to pull out in a time of need. These words could be my hug to her at 2 a.m. when she was up for the twelfth time that night to feed the baby.

Okay, I can't imagine at that moment she would go digging for my note, but perhaps later. Perhaps, she'd read my "word hug," and it would give her a little boost to get through the next struggle.

My helpful husband suggested that I had identified a problem that wasn't just something I had been through, or that my friend would go through. If the love from one friend could help a mom in need, why not the love from her entire support group? As fellow mothers, partners, friends, or family, we all have love to share with the special new moms in our lives, and in that way we can all be Mommy Motivators.

Introduction

What is Mommy Motivators?

Mommy Motivators is a structured journal meant to be passed around among friends, relatives, partners and other individuals trusted by a soon-to-be mom. These people are to share stories, wisdom, and simple understanding related to certain milestones in a new mother's life. In particularly difficult times, the recipient mom can reference these heartfelt, handwritten notes for guidance, inspiration, or simply that reassuring feeling of knowing "I'm not alone in this."

Why do we need Mommy Motivators?

Being a parent is an incredibly rewarding job, but a difficult one as well. It's also a job that comes without any training whatsoever, and yet we expect ourselves to immediately become "employee of the year"! Thanks to social media, we see so many others in this world with the same job, and they are seemingly excelling! It's to be expected that people want to share the best moments of parenthood online and with the public. However, one would hope most decent people wouldn't want other mothers comparing themselves to their posts and then feeling bad about themselves. Each person has so much more to share about their story and their journey than what we post publicly, and Mommy Motivators is a wonderful opportunity to share something about ourselves that isn't an image of perfection. Instead of perpetuating the image of the superhero mom who can do it all, let's share among people we trust the reality of motherhood, which is mostly glorious but sometimes includes tough days where we feel like we're falling short. On those days, one mommy can use her stories and experience to uplift and motivate another.

How does it work?

Mommy Motivators can be filled out by one particularly ambitious friend/relative, but ideally multiple individuals would contribute to this journal before gifting to the intended mom. It could be passed among a circle of friends over time, or it might be an excellent baby shower activity. The more input given, the more likely a new mom will find a note (or notes) that she really connects with during the different difficult circumstances she may encounter. Even after baby has arrived, you may want to check in with mom to see if there's any part of the journal that she would like more help or encouragement with, especially as parenting challenges change over time as our children grow.

There are additional sections for mom to fill in, allowing her an opportunity to reflect, vent, meditate, or just do something for herself for a few minutes.

If you want to help even more, go to the "Pledgistry" pages to pledge additional love and assistance to the special mommy.

How do I fill out Mommy Motivators?

Find a section (or sections) of the journal that you have strong memories of or feelings toward, or if you are not a mother yourself, ones that you feel particularly drawn to. Write a handwritten note to mom; consider what she needs to hear most during this time or what would have helped you when you were in that situation.

> • *Be Specific:* Hearing stories about what others have been through can help mom relate; even though everyone's story will be different, many of the circumstances, if not feelings, may overlap.

> • B*e Vulnerable:* People tend to show the best part of their lives to others, especially when it comes to social media.

There is a lot of "greatness" out there for moms to compare themselves with, and very little reality. Do your best to be open and honest—you don't have to sign your name to your note(s) if you don't want to.

• *Be Tailored:* The topics are intended to be broad enough for application to most mothers, but your input allows the book to be customized to this unique person. Know your audience. If you know this person has decided to formula feed, it's unlikely that information/stories about breastfeeding will be directly applicable.

• *Be Helpful (but be wise about it):* If you have been through motherhood you know that everyone has advice to shell out, and now you have advice to share too! Offering words of advice can be helpful, but be careful about offering very specific unsolicited advice that could be misconstrued or hurtful if it does not recognize the uniqueness of every mother's situation. For example, imagine a new mom confiding to her mom friends about issues with her milk supply. If one chimes in about how she has had freezer full of milk ever since she started drinking sports drinks, this comment might not be received well depending on the audience. Staying hydrated seems like good advice for pretty much any situation, but if advice comes with a boast or simplifies the struggles others, you may do more harm than good. This isn't the place to needlessly scare mom, provide unwelcome advice, or to insert a subtle brag.

If your message comes from the heart and with the best of intentions, you will be sharing a wonderful gift.

What if I'm uncomfortable getting so personal?

There are probably some things mothers have been through that they are uncomfortable sharing with others, no matter how helpful it might be to be so candid. It's great to try to put yourself out there, but if it's too difficult to share then don't.

Remember that you can sign your name to your notes if you wish, but in some ways, anonymity can be even better and remove any reader bias.

The things you write in this journal are meant for one particular mommy to read, but to get the input and motivation from multiple sources it could at some point be in front of many people. Fellow Motivators are encouraged to focus on their own writing (in other words, don't be nosy). However, if you're okay with sharing something with the mommy but worried about other readers snooping on your thoughts, you could fold the page(s) you wrote inward. No, this can't stop anyone from unfolding, but it is an extra reminder to everyone's conscience.

How do I use Mommy Motivators?

If you're the recipient of this journal, keep this in a place you can access it often. Take a mental note of the contents section now, so that you hopefully think back to this journal when you find yourself in these scenarios.

You may be eager to read all the notes right away but remember that they will hold so much more value to you as time goes on. When you do read your journal, do so without judgment of yourself or others. Not everyone's words will be perfect or exactly what you need each time, but hopefully the love and concern that they took time to pour out to you on these pages is always evident.

There are also template pages for you as a new mom to fill out, and you can do so multiple times within each section (after all, each topic is not something that will just occur to you once). Your time is lacking, but the prompts are short and allow you to take a well-deserved moment to reflect on yourself and track your journey, maybe even find a little self-motivation!

What is "Pledgistry"?

You may be fortunate enough to have many wonderful people give you many wonderful things as gifts for you and the baby. We hold baby showers because we care about other women and their journey into motherhood, and we recognize the financial strain that can come with inviting a little one into your life. However, some of the best gifts that a new mother can receive are acts of love. A couple of weeks after my baby was born, a friend stopped by to give us some baked breakfast treats. She simply dropped them off and left; she did not expect to be entertained or to see the baby. Shortly after I returned to work, a coworker brought me several freezer meals to help me adjust to my new "working mom" schedule. These things helped me survive. My friends provided nourishment for my body and my heart.

Despite this, there were other times when I struggled. I needed someone to hold the baby while I did the laundry. I needed someone to do the laundry. I needed a girlfriend to talk to. I needed a moment. So many people at some point or another said to me, "let me know if you need anything," but I didn't call them. Sometimes I didn't know what I needed, or it was too difficult to verbalize. Other times, I didn't know if what I wanted to ask for seemed silly, or if I really should be asking for help at all.   Mostly I just never thought to ask for help. It's not easy to reach out or call in a favor that was offered briefly over a casual conversation several months ago.

<u>Pledgistry is a registry of all the things loved ones pledge to do for mom.</u> These items are specific and something you'd be more than

happy to do for mom. Don't feel obligated to pledge anything! Odds are you're probably at or planning to attend a baby shower for which you've already spent money, and you're filling in this book – isn't that enough? Absolutely! But if you find yourself saying "let me know if you need anything," and you really do wish you could do more, this is for you.

How do I use Pledgistry?

If you're mom, you may want to fill out the first page of the Pledgistry section in case some individuals who may want to help don't have all your contact information.

As a Mommy Motivator, simply go to the Pledgistry section of this journal and pledge to help the new mom by providing food, your time, or an ear to listen. Fill out the basic prompts for the pledge. Sometime after the baby arrives, make sure to coordinate with mom how you can give the assistance you pledged. Be careful not to overwhelm her in the first few weeks, and then forget about her later—motherhood never ends.

Can You Sum This Up?

If you plan on using this book as a baby shower activity, you don't have time for every participant to read this entire introduction. See the next page for Quick Instructions, which can be shared aloud with a group. Or, you may wish to visit our website for a printout of the Quick Instructions at www.mommotivators.com.

Quick Instructions

This book is an opportunity for you to share stories, wisdom, and simple understanding related to certain motherhood milestones. In difficult times, mom can reference these heartfelt, handwritten notes for guidance, inspiration, or simply that wonderful feeling of knowing "I'm not alone in this."

1. Flip through this book to find the lined pages "For the Mommy Motivators" and pick a topic or topics that you are drawn to.   Be careful not to fill out the prompted pages that are specifically "For Mom…"

2. Write a note to mom that you think would help her through tough times related to this topic. Keep the following in mind:

• Remember to tailor your note to this special woman.

• Don't be afraid to be vulnerable and specific when sharing your own experiences.

• Be careful to avoid wording that could be misconstrued or hurtful.

• You don't have to sign your name, and you can fold the pages inward if you are concerned about privacy.

3. If you'd like to help even more, flip to the back and fill out a section of "Pledgistry" to pledge a service or act of kindness to help this wonderful new mother.

Thank you for sharing your love, stories, and insight, and for providing mommy motivation!

*The beginning is the most
important part of a work*

Plato

When You're in the First Few Weeks

The first few weeks of motherhood are filled with excitement, good or bad. There is a new person in your life, and you are flooded with new emotions and responsibilities. Unless you had a surrogate or adopted, you are also recovering physically while trying to care for your baby, which can mean aches and pains, sickness, and/or weird hormonal changes. Some women may be blessed with helpful visitors and a supportive partner, while others may be either physically or emotionally on their own. Even with an excellent support system, there can be feelings of uncertainty and inadequacy around being a new mom.

Regardless of every new mother's situation, the first few weeks are unlike any other time she's ever had in her life. You are a mom – that's a powerful, joyful, and scary feeling! At the same time, your needs take a backseat, and your ability to sleep, shower, or use the bathroom in peace seems to drop off the face of the earth. It's a major adjustment and one that you won't get the hang of right away, so make sure you give yourself a break. The first few weeks are a great time to forget about everything that's on your normal "to-do" list, ignore any negative thoughts or worries, and simply enjoy some cuddles with the beautiful person that is a part of your new reality.

This may be easier said than done. Relaxing and living in the moment is a challenge when you have a new life to care for (and you may not know the first thing about how to do it)! Some worries and concerns are very real. Some are unnecessarily accentuated by our inexperience, physical recovery, temporary baby blues, or possibly a more severe mood disorder. Your friends and family may be able to help you through tough times and soothe your concerns in the first few weeks and those to come, but for those who may be experiencing postpartum depression, seeking the additional help of a medical professional is best. Regardless of your physical, emotional and mental state, admitting to any feeling besides pure ecstasy after having a baby is something many moms may feel ashamed of but shouldn't. It does not negate your love.

For the Mommy Motivators....

When You're in the First Few Weeks

_____

_____

_____

_____

_____

_____

_____

_____

_____

_____

_____

_____

_____

_____

_____

_____

_____

_____

_____

_____

For the Mommy Motivators

_____

_____

_____

_____

_____

_____

_____

_____

_____

_____

_____

_____

_____

_____

_____

_____

_____

_____

_____

_____

_____

_____

_____

_____

_____

_____

_____

_____

_____

_____

_____

_____

_____

_____

_____

_____

_____

_____

_____

_____

_____

_____

_____

_____

_____

_____

_____

_____

_____

_____

For the Mommy Motivators

_____

_____

_____

_____

_____

_____

_____

_____

_____

_____

_____

_____

_____

_____

_____

_____

_____

_____

_____

_____

_____

_____

_____

_____

_____

_____

_____

_____

For Mom...   When You're in the First Few Weeks

Date: _____

Right now I am feeling

_____

_____

_____

_____

_____

_____

The hardest part is

_____

_____

_____

_____

_____

_____

The best part is

_____

_____

_____

_____

_____

_____

Baby's Age _____

I'm so appreciative for

_____

_____

_____

_____

_____

_____

I feel I need

_____

_____

_____

_____

_____

_____

If I went through this again, I would tell myself

_____

_____

_____

_____

_____

_____

For Mom...   When You're in the First Few Weeks

Date: _____

Right now I am feeling

_____

_____

_____

_____

_____

_____

The hardest part is

_____

_____

_____

_____

_____

The best part is

_____

_____

_____

_____

_____

_____

Baby's Age _____

I'm so appreciative for

_____

_____

_____

_____

_____

_____

I feel I need

_____

_____

_____

_____

_____

_____

If I went through this again, I would tell myself

_____

_____

_____

_____

_____

_____

Date: _____

Right now I am feeling

_____

_____

_____

_____

_____

_____

The hardest part is

_____

_____

_____

_____

_____

_____

The best part is

_____

_____

_____

_____

_____

_____

Baby's Age _____

I'm so appreciative for

_____
_____
_____
_____
_____
_____

I feel I need

_____
_____
_____
_____
_____

If I went through this again, I would tell myself

_____
_____
_____
_____
_____
_____

Life is a flower of which love is the honey

Victor Hugo

When You're Having Feeding Troubles

Despite it being a very personal decision, a lot of mothers will find that all sorts of people are super interested in how you feed your baby. Some people ask just because they want to be supportive, or to make sure they get you the right baby shower gift. At another extreme, there are people who make it their personal mission to make sure everyone chooses the exact same feeding option as them, or at least make them feel bad for not doing so. There are many educated resources out there to help mothers make the right decision for themselves and their children. There is also a lot of pressure around this topic and a lot of information out there that can be scary, judgmental, or flat-out wrong.

This section is not meant to influence mom's decision on this matter, but to help her along whatever route she chooses. Even once you've chosen how you plan to feed, there are plenty of different obstacles you can encounter. Your plans may have to change in order to meet your baby's needs. Perhaps you or your baby ends up with a condition that makes breastfeeding difficult or impossible, or that brand of formula you stocked up on doesn't suit his stomach. It's amazing that women's bodies can produce milk, but it's also a modern miracle that we have formula!

Relatively speaking, the period of bottle-feeding or breastfeeding will be a very short time in a child's life. Moving further into the future with solid food and beyond, there are different problems with getting children to eat vegetables or develop manners, and mothers can grapple with how to provide nutritious meals amid everything else going on. Some moms get joy from making their own organic baby food and creating lunchbox masterpieces while others are just happy to put food on the table. As a Mommy Motivator, remember the struggles you came across and how you tackled them, or what you wish someone would have told you. Regardless of however mom decides to feed baby, let's feed her with love.

For the Mommy Motivators....

When You're Having Feeding Troubles

_____

_____

_____

_____

_____

_____

_____

_____

_____

_____

_____

_____

_____

_____

_____

_____

_____

_____

_____

_____

_____

For the Mommy Motivators

_____

_____

_____

_____

_____

_____

_____

_____

_____

_____

_____

_____

_____

_____

_____

_____

_____

_____

_____

_____

_____

_____

_____

_____

_____

_____

_____

_____

_____

_____

_____

_____

_____

_____

_____

_____

_____

_____

_____

_____

_____

_____

_____

_____

_____

_____

_____

_____

_____

For the Mommy Motivators

_____

_____

_____

_____

_____

_____

_____

_____

_____

_____

_____

_____

_____

_____

_____

_____

_____

_____

_____

_____

_____

_____

_____

Date: _____

Right now I am feeling

_____

_____

_____

_____

_____

The hardest part is

_____

_____

_____

_____

_____

The best part is

_____

_____

_____

_____

_____

Baby's Age:_____

I'm so appreciative for

_____

_____

_____

_____

_____

_____

I feel I need

_____

_____

_____

_____

_____

_____

If I went through this again, I would tell myself

_____

_____

_____

_____

_____

_____

For Mom...　　　　　　　When You're Having Feeding Troubles

Date: _____

Right now I am feeling

_____

_____

_____

_____

_____

The hardest part is

_____

_____

_____

_____

_____

The best part is

_____

_____

_____

_____

_____

Baby's Age:_____

I'm so appreciative for

_____

_____

_____

_____

_____

_____

I feel I need

_____

_____

_____

_____

_____

_____

If I went through this again, I would tell myself

_____

_____

_____

_____

_____

_____

For Mom... When You're Having Feeding Troubles

Date: _____

Right now I am feeling

_____
_____
_____
_____
_____

The hardest part is

_____
_____
_____
_____
_____

The best part is

_____
_____
_____
_____
_____

Baby's Age:_____

I'm so appreciative for

_____

_____

_____

_____

_____

_____

I feel I need

_____

_____

_____

_____

_____

_____

If I went through this again, I would tell myself

_____

_____

_____

_____

_____

_____

Patience is bitter, but its fruit
is sweet

Jean-Jacques Rousseau

When You Haven't Slept in Weeks

A favorite question to ask new parents is often, "is the baby sleeping through the night yet?" Perhaps some well-meaning people want to know if *you* are sleeping through the night, and if you are not, they might then wish to extend their sympathy and understanding. However, it typically feels like a test, and the "yet" in particular seems to imply that the answer should be "yes" by now, whether it was asked at one year or one week! Failing this test can often result in unsolicited advice or even someone telling you that what you've been doing is wrong. Others may share how they successfully managed to get their child to sleep, but very few go the road of empathy first or recognize the time and number of failures it can take to achieve sleeping success!

Most people, if they are not sleeping at night, do in fact wish they could be sleeping at night. More than likely, parents who are struggling with sleep have tried a multitude of different things, but to no avail. If there were a simple answer, there wouldn't be so many books on the topic! If you choose to share advice on this topic, or if you are the recipient of this advice, try to remember that every child and situation is different. Most importantly, keep in mind that sleep-deprived parents most likely do not feel well physically and may be experiencing feelings of failure and frustration – a little motivation can go a long way.

No matter your situation, at some point you will struggle with sleep. Whether your baby seems to eat every 2 hours for a year, your 4-year-old has night terrors, or your teenager stays out past curfew, there will always be some time when they will keep you up at night. Whatever the cause or length of your sleep debt, the misery is a shared experience for all parents to some extent. You may end up with a pretty great sleeper, but still suffer from fatigue due to your new lifestyle. Even when you get time to yourself, it can be challenging to choose rest when there are bottles to clean, laundry to do, or toys to pick up. It's important to give yourself permission to rest when you can, so you have energy to be your best self. In the midst of sleep deprivation and fatigue, it seems like it will never end. It's a fog that won't seem to clear, but just know that this is not your new reality forever. This time will pass, and one day, someday, you will sleep again!

For the Mommy Motivators....

When You Haven't Slept in Weeks

_____

_____

_____

_____

_____

_____

_____

_____

_____

_____

_____

_____

_____

_____

_____

_____

_____

_____

_____

_____

_____

_____

For the Mommy Motivators

For the Mommy Motivators

_____

_____

_____

_____

_____

_____

_____

_____

_____

_____

_____

_____

_____

_____

_____

_____

_____

_____

_____

_____

_____

_____

_____

_____

_____

For Mom...   When You Haven't Slept in Weeks

Date: _____

Right now I am feeling

_____
_____
_____
_____
_____

The hardest part is

_____
_____
_____
_____
_____

The best part is

_____
_____
_____
_____
_____

Baby's Age:_____

I'm so appreciative for

_____

_____

_____

_____

_____

_____

I feel I need

_____

_____

_____

_____

_____

_____

If I went through this again, I would tell myself

_____

_____

_____

_____

_____

Date: _____

Right now I am feeling

_____

_____

_____

_____

_____

The hardest part is

_____

_____

_____

_____

_____

The best part is

_____

_____

_____

_____

_____

Baby's Age:_____

I'm so appreciative for

_____

_____

_____

_____

_____

_____

I feel I need

_____

_____

_____

_____

_____

_____

If I went through this again, I would tell myself

_____

_____

_____

_____

_____

_____

For Mom...   When You Haven't Slept in Weeks

Date: _____

Right now I am feeling

_____

_____

_____

_____

_____

The hardest part is

_____

_____

_____

_____

_____

The best part is

_____

_____

_____

_____

_____

Baby's Age:_____

I'm so appreciative for

_____

_____

_____

_____

_____

_____

I feel I need

_____

_____

_____

_____

_____

_____

If I went through this again, I would tell myself

_____

_____

_____

_____

_____

_____

*Life is a balance of holding on
and letting go*

Rumi

When You're Adjusting to Your New Role

Everyone must adjust to their new role as a parent, and this can be a struggle for many different reasons. One particular thing that may be difficult to deal with is a feeling of loss of identity. For those who feel that, this feeling is okay—it doesn't mean they don't want to be mothers, or that they truly long for their pre-baby life. It's just simply tough, and you might feel a little lost as all focus shifts to your child. The reality is that one day our babies will grow up and hopefully they will be able to make a life of their own where they no longer need to entirely rely on us. Therefore, while a baby does require most of our time and energy to care for, it's important not to let motherhood become your entire identity. Our minds encourage us to find a little alone time while simultaneously making us feel like we should watch our children's every move. If you're in a relationship, this will also change things between you as you both evolve from partners to parents. While you try to care for your new love, that first partnership somehow still needs to be nurtured and given attention. We need to allow ourselves to take time for just us, as well as time for our other relationships, and remember that we will be better parents for it.

At the same time, you do have a new role that you must take on, and it involves a lot of uncertainty and lack of control over your everyday life. It may seem that some mothers are naturals, while others second guess everything. Some may struggle with issues that prevent them from making that immediate expected connection with the child that they so desired. There are women with children who would say they were never a "kid-person" before they had a baby and might still not be! All these people still want to be good mothers for their children and want to grow in their role. If you find yourself struggling, remember that it's important to focus on who you are and what that person looks like as a mom, rather than trying to grow into an idealized version of motherhood that you think you should be. You're still you, and that's the person your child needs.

For the Mommy Motivators....

When You're Adjusting to Your New Role

_____

_____

_____

_____

_____

_____

_____

_____

_____

_____

_____

_____

_____

_____

_____

_____

_____

_____

_____

_____

_____

_____

_____

For the Mommy Motivators

_____

_____

_____

_____

_____

_____

_____

_____

_____

_____

_____

_____

_____

_____

_____

_____

_____

_____

_____

_____

_____

_____

_____

_____

_____
_____
_____
_____
_____
_____
_____
_____
_____
_____
_____
_____
_____
_____
_____
_____
_____
_____
_____
_____
_____
_____
_____
_____
_____
_____
_____
_____

For the Mommy Motivators

_____

_____

_____

_____

_____

_____

_____

_____

_____

_____

_____

_____

_____

_____

_____

_____

_____

_____

_____

_____

_____

_____

_____

_____

_____

_____

_____

For Mom...   When You're Adjusting to Your New Role

Date: _____

Right now I am feeling

_____

_____

_____

_____

_____

_____

The hardest part is

_____

_____

_____

_____

_____

The best part is

_____

_____

_____

_____

_____

Baby's Age _____

I'm so appreciative for

_____

_____

_____

_____

_____

I feel I need

_____

_____

_____

_____

_____

If I went through this again, I would tell myself

_____

_____

_____

_____

_____

For Mom...   When You're Adjusting to Your New Role

Date: _____

Right now I am feeling

_____

_____

_____

_____

_____

The hardest part is

_____

_____

_____

_____

_____

The best part is

_____

_____

_____

_____

_____

Baby's Age _____

I'm so appreciative for

_____

_____

_____

_____

_____

I feel I need

_____

_____

_____

_____

_____

If I went through this again, I would tell myself

_____

_____

_____

_____

_____

For Mom…   When You're Adjusting to Your New Role

Date: _____

Right now I am feeling

_____

_____

_____

_____

_____

The hardest part is

_____

_____

_____

_____

_____

The best part is

_____

_____

_____

_____

_____

Baby's Age _____

I'm so appreciative for

_____

_____

_____

_____

_____

_____

I feel I need

_____

_____

_____

_____

_____

_____

If I went through this again, I would tell myself

_____

_____

_____

_____

_____

_____

*For every minute you are
angry, you give up sixty
seconds of happiness*

Ralph Waldo Emerson

When You Don't Recognize Your Body

Women sacrifice a lot when they become mothers, but the first thing to change is our bodies. Whether you were sick every day or glowing, enjoyed all the changes or felt monstrously out of control, you certainly experience some impact to your body before baby has even arrived.

Afterward, many women are anxious for the time when they will look like they used to. The unfair reality is that some people will find that goal easily attainable, while others will feel like their body has changed forever. Celebrities keep trying to outdo each other with who can produce the fastest post-baby body magazine cover, and we are left to wonder if we've failed for not doing the same.

Besides weight gain, different experiences can yield different results in other areas such as breastfeeding or recovery from childbirth. Or perhaps each subsequent baby leads to a different shape altogether. Sleepless nights may start to distort the face looking back at you in the mirror, and time for self-care becomes very limited. We are so much more than our appearance, but everyone wants to feel and look their best. For each mom, your body will be different from your "before picture" in some way because it has gone through a life-changing and incredible process of producing and raising a child. The focus for all mothers should not be on resenting the new differences, but glorifying our bodies and finding gratitude for the labor our bodies have gone through and the lives they have helped create.

For the Mommy Motivators....

When You Don't Recognize Your Body

_____

_____

_____

_____

_____

_____

_____

_____

_____

_____

_____

_____

_____

_____

_____

_____

_____

_____

_____

_____

_____

_____

For the Mommy Motivators

_____
_____
_____
_____
_____
_____
_____
_____
_____
_____
_____
_____
_____
_____
_____
_____
_____
_____
_____
_____
_____
_____
_____
_____
_____
_____
_____

_____

_____

_____

_____

_____

_____

_____

_____

_____

_____

_____

_____

_____

_____

_____

_____

_____

_____

_____

_____

_____

_____

_____

_____

_____

_____

_____

_____

_____

_____

_____

_____

_____

_____

_____

_____

_____

_____

_____

_____

_____

_____

_____

_____

_____

_____

_____

Date: _____

Right now I am feeling

_____

_____

_____

_____

_____

_____

The hardest part is

_____

_____

_____

_____

_____

The best part is

_____

_____

_____

_____

_____

Baby's Age _____

I'm so appreciative for

_____

_____

_____

_____

_____

I feel I need

_____

_____

_____

_____

_____

If I went through this again, I would tell myself

_____

_____

_____

_____

_____

For Mom...　　　　When You Don't Recognize Your Body

Date: _____

Right now I am feeling

_____
_____
_____
_____
_____

The hardest part is

_____
_____
_____
_____
_____

The best part is

_____
_____
_____
_____
_____

Baby's Age _____

I'm so appreciative for

_____
_____
_____
_____
_____

I feel I need

_____
_____
_____
_____
_____

If I went through this again, I would tell myself

_____
_____
_____
_____
_____

Date: _____

Right now I am feeling

_____

_____

_____

_____

_____

_____

The hardest part is

_____

_____

_____

_____

_____

The best part is

_____

_____

_____

_____

_____

Baby's Age _____

I'm so appreciative for

_____
_____
_____
_____
_____

I feel I need

_____
_____
_____
_____

If I went through this again, I would tell myself

_____
_____
_____
_____
_____

There is nothing on this earth more to be prized than true friendship

Thomas Aquinas

When You're Feeling Lonely

Early motherhood can be exciting, and it certainly doesn't seem like you should have any reason to feel lonely – there are often many visitors and, regardless of that, you have this new addition to your life! Isn't your little one the best company to have? Given that it's pretty much a one-way relationship initially, perhaps not. Your new little companion has a lot of needs but doesn't give much back in the way of conversation just yet. No matter what level of support you may have, there will still be times when you feel like you are on your own and struggling with it. There may be times when you miss your old social life, and you may feel like you are losing touch with some of your friends. If you are fortunate enough to have a significant other by your side, you may still feel alone emotionally at times and your new dynamic may put a strain on your relationship. Some family members or friends may not seem to understand how you feel or what you need most. Even years down the road when your child or children are older and you have formed more of a relationship with them, you may be dishing out loads of hugs and kisses one minute and the next feeling a bit isolated. Perhaps some women would feel guilt over this, asking, "Aren't my children enough?" No matter how great they are, certainly it's not fair to your children to expect them to fill all your social needs.

Feelings of loneliness don't always come from physical isolation, but also through difficult experiences or parenting challenges that we think others would not relate to or would judge us for. Perhaps the notes in this journal will help you to see that this is not the case.

For the Mommy Motivators....

When You're Feeling Lonely

_____

_____

_____

_____

_____

_____

_____

_____

_____

_____

_____

_____

_____

_____

_____

_____

_____

_____

_____

_____

For the Mommy Motivators

_____

_____

_____

_____

_____

_____

_____

_____

_____

_____

_____

_____

_____

_____

_____

_____

_____

_____

_____

_____

_____

_____

_____

_____

_____

_____

_____

_____

_____

_____

_____

_____

_____

_____

_____

_____

_____

_____

_____

_____

_____

_____

_____

_____

_____

_____

_____

_____

For the Mommy Motivators

_____

_____

_____

_____

_____

_____

_____

_____

_____

_____

_____

_____

_____

_____

_____

_____

_____

_____

_____

_____

_____

_____

Date: _____

Right now I am feeling

_____

_____

_____

_____

_____

_____

The hardest part is

_____

_____

_____

_____

_____

_____

The best part is

_____

_____

_____

_____

_____

_____

Baby's Age _____

I'm so appreciative for

_____

_____

_____

_____

_____

I feel I need

_____

_____

_____

_____

_____

If I went through this again, I would tell myself

_____

_____

_____

_____

_____

For Mom...   When You're Feeling Lonely

Date: _____

Right now I am feeling

_____

_____

_____

_____

_____

The hardest part is

_____

_____

_____

_____

_____

The best part is

_____

_____

_____

_____

_____

Baby's Age _____

I'm so appreciative for

_____

_____

_____

_____

_____

I feel I need

_____

_____

_____

_____

_____

If I went through this again, I would tell myself

_____

_____

_____

_____

_____

Date: _____

Right now I am feeling

_____

_____

_____

_____

_____

The hardest part is

_____

_____

_____

_____

_____

The best part is

_____

_____

_____

_____

_____

Baby's Age _____

I'm so appreciative for

_____

_____

_____

_____

_____

I feel I need

_____

_____

_____

_____

_____

If I went through this again, I would tell myself

_____

_____

_____

_____

_____

Don't judge each day by the harvest you reap but by the seeds that you plant

Robert Louis Stevenson

When You Struggle with Work

This section is meant to encompass all areas of "work" for a mother, which includes the job title of stay-at-home mom. Being a stay-at-home mom was once the only option for a woman, but times have changed. It's wonderful to live in a time with more career opportunities than ever for women, while also living in a time where women (and men) still have the freedom to choose to stay at home with their children when it's financially feasible. However, this choice to stay at home seems to come with some different expectations these days. Stay-at-home mothers may feel a certain responsibility to get involved in everything and get their kids involved as well. They're not a "working mom," so shouldn't they have time to join the PTA, volunteer, take the kids to music/story time, have a pristine home, create healthy yet unique meals, all while raising perfect children? Stay-at-home moms are always on call and never get to leave their "office." They may sometimes feel like the work they are doing is not valued. Families with a stay-at-home dad may have similar experiences, on top of facing some other criticism.

On the other hand, working moms can feel conflicted about not being home (or feel guilty or looked down on for not having that calling to be at home). Finding the right childcare and leaving your children for a good portion of the day with someone else presents its own logistical and emotional problems. Opportunities for women in the workforce have grown tremendously, but these opportunities don't necessarily create automatic satisfaction despite appearances of "having it all." Finding the right balance between home and work life is a difficult task for all parents, and new mothers may have an especially tough time being thrust into this task after a particularly brief and abruptly ending maternity leave. Others may feel like the choice is made for them, with finances or personal situations making staying at home a non-option.

You may also do something in between these options with part-time work or may decide to make a change that is only temporary until your kids reach a certain age. Regardless of what you do, even when you feel entirely secure in your decision and know that it is the best thing for you and your family, it can still be very hard to find any solution that feels 100% right all the time. Women (and men) sometimes must defend their choices on this matter, to friends, family, coworkers, and even to themselves when things get tough. There are so many feelings and problems involved with each situation, whether you are always home with your children, or you have a job that takes you halfway around the world from you family. Feeling supported in this matter and reassured that you can be a great mom in any situation can go a long way.

When You Struggle With Work

Its getting close to time to head back to work! Not only will this transition be difficult in normal circumstances, but w/ covid school is going to look alot different this year. I'm teaching 3rd grade which will be a whole new set of challenges. Theres going to be a million rules tied to COVID and its just going to be such a new and tricky beast. I am feeling SAD to leave my baby but I really trust Danielle and I do feel like she is the most perfect fit. I know she will love and care for Finley as her own. I'm also worried about actually contracting the virus and giving it to Finley, but I guess we will cross that bridge when we get to it. I know

the Lord is with our family.
It is helpful to know
that all mamas struggle
with the decision of
back to work vs. stay
home, but this does
feel like the right choice
for our family for right
now.

For the Mommy Motivators

_____

_____

_____

_____

_____

_____

_____

_____

_____

_____

_____

_____

_____

_____

_____

_____

_____

_____

_____

_____

_____

_____

_____

Date: _____

Right now I am feeling

_____

_____

_____

_____

_____

The hardest part is

_____

_____

_____

_____

_____

The best part is

_____

_____

_____

_____

_____

Baby's Age _____

I'm so appreciative for

_____

_____

_____

_____

_____

I feel I need

_____

_____

_____

_____

_____

If I went through this again, I would tell myself

_____

_____

_____

_____

_____

Date: _____

Right now I am feeling

_____

_____

_____

_____

_____

_____

The hardest part is

_____

_____

_____

_____

_____

The best part is

_____

_____

_____

_____

_____

Baby's Age _____

I'm so appreciative for

_____
_____
_____
_____
_____

I feel I need

_____
_____
_____
_____
_____

If I went through this again, I would tell myself

_____
_____
_____
_____
_____
_____

Date: _____

Right now I am feeling

_____

_____

_____

_____

_____

The hardest part is

_____

_____

_____

_____

_____

The best part is

_____

_____

_____

_____

_____

Baby's Age _____

I'm so appreciative for

_____

_____

_____

_____

_____

_____

I feel I need

_____

_____

_____

_____

_____

_____

If I went through this again, I would tell myself

_____

_____

_____

_____

_____

_____

Love inspires, illumines,
designates, and leads the way

Mary Baker Eddy

When You Feel Lost or Inadequate

Sometimes birth experiences don't go as planned or breastfeeding doesn't work out as you wished, and a part of you might feel like you've failed. Maybe someone makes a snide comment about you wanting to formula feed or how often your baby cries. You may even be your own worst critic, judging yourself for the state of your home or your unsuccessful attempts at swaddling. When a child comes along, so too come a lot of questions, and you may feel frustrated for not knowing all the answers, whether it is the first week of motherhood or your child's first week of high school.

If you go looking for comfort or answers out on the Internet, you may walk away feeling much worse. Just as anyone who's ever looked up the search results for their mild symptoms could almost always diagnose themselves with some terrible disease, a mom or dad with questions for the world wide web could very easily diagnose themselves as a terrible parent. You may know deep down that this negative content is not worth listening to, and that there is a lot of other good advice and feedback out there, but it's often the hurtful words that stick with us. Even those people who you trust and are not hiding behind a screen can say things that cause pain or make you feel less than, whether intentional or not.

With everyone sharing all their best moments on social media these days, the Internet is also a great place to go if you want to feel lost and completely inadequate as you compare yourself with everyone else's high points. Avoiding the Internet won't necessarily leave you immune to comparisons with those around you or what you envisioned for yourself. Even the most confident women will wonder if they've done something wrong at some point.

As human beings, we are all flawed, and likely you will not make perfect decisions throughout your entire life – that doesn't change just because you become a parent either. Every job you've ever had has come with mistakes or things you wish you did better. Reflections on those experiences allow you to evolve and become even better, yet likely there were many positive things you did every day that just don't stand out as much. If you feel lost or inadequate, congratulate yourself on caring enough to reflect on your role as a parent; you'll learn so much from this experience, but also try to think of all the positives you do that may not always stick out in your mind. There may be a lot of information, images, and people out there that don't always make you feel your best, but you are the best person for this job.

For the Mommy Motivators....

When You Feel Lost or Inadequate

_____

_____

_____

_____

_____

_____

_____

_____

_____

_____

_____

_____

_____

_____

_____

_____

_____

_____

_____

_____

For the Mommy Motivators

_____

_____

_____

_____

_____

_____

_____

_____

_____

_____

_____

_____

_____

_____

_____

_____

_____

_____

_____

_____

_____

_____

_____

_____

_____

_____

_____

_____

_____

_____

_____

_____

_____

_____

_____

_____

_____

_____

_____

_____

_____

_____

_____

_____

_____

_____

_____

_____

_____

_____

_____

_____

For the Mommy Motivators

_____

_____

_____

_____

_____

_____

_____

_____

_____

_____

_____

_____

_____

_____

_____

_____

_____

_____

_____

_____

_____

_____

_____

Date: _____

Right now I am feeling

_____

_____

_____

_____

_____

The hardest part is

_____

_____

_____

_____

_____

The best part is

_____

_____

_____

_____

_____

Baby's Age _____

I'm so appreciative for

_____

_____

_____

_____

_____

_____

I feel I need

_____

_____

_____

_____

_____

_____

If I went through this again, I would tell myself

_____

_____

_____

_____

_____

_____

For Mom...   *When You Feel Lost or Inadequate*

Date: _____

Right now I am feeling

_____

_____

_____

_____

_____

The hardest part is

_____

_____

_____

_____

_____

The best part is

_____

_____

_____

_____

_____

Baby's Age _____

I'm so appreciative for

_____

_____

_____

_____

_____

I feel I need

_____

_____

_____

_____

_____

If I went through this again, I would tell myself

_____

_____

_____

_____

_____

Date: _____

Right now I am feeling

_____

_____

_____

_____

_____

The hardest part is

_____

_____

_____

_____

_____

The best part is

_____

_____

_____

_____

_____

Baby's Age _____

I'm so appreciative for

_____

_____

_____

_____

_____

I feel I need

_____

_____

_____

_____

_____

If I went through this again, I would tell myself

_____

_____

_____

_____

_____

_____

Happiness never decreases by being shared

Guatama Budah

"Pledgistry"

A baby registry is helpful in that it lets mom's generous friends and family members know what items she would prefer and keeps track of everything to make sure that the baby doesn't end up with five bottle warmers. Every single gift we receive is a blessing to help us with our children, but not everything of value needs to come with a price tag. One thing you might wish you could have registered for is a nice peaceful bath and a nap!

Pledgistry is like a registry of all the things everyone may wish to pledge to do for mom. Simple things like a meal or snack, a helping hand, or a supportive phone call. Unlike bottle warmers, you can never get too many of these pledge gifts! When we take care of ourselves and our fellow moms, we are better for it and better for our children.

If you'd like to make a pledge to help mom, make sure you know how to get in touch with her when the time comes. Here's mom's info:

Mom's Phone Number: _____

Mom's Email: _____

Mom's Address: _____

Prefers: ☐ Text ☐ Phone Calls ☐ Email

Allergies / Dietary Restrictions: _____

_____

I Pledge to...

Feed You and Your Family

I want to bring you food, because food is love! Maybe I will bring you a freezer meal that is simple to heat up. Perhaps I will bring you a home cooked meal piping hot! It could be baked goods, or just some healthy cut up fruit. Whatever it is, I will tell you in advance. We can coordinate a drop-off. I will bring you food with no expectations of being entertained. I just want to take care of you, whether you need me in the first few weeks or down the road.

Name: _____

I would like to bring you _____

_____

Name: _____

I would like to bring you _____

_____

Name: _____

I would like to bring you _____

_____

Name: _____

I would like to bring you _____

_____

Name: _____

I would like to bring you _____

_____

Name: _____

I would like to bring you _____

_____

Name: _____

I would like to bring you _____

_____

Name: _____

I would like to bring you _____

_____

Name: _____

I would like to bring you _____

_____

Name: _____

I would like to bring you _____

_____

Name: _____

I would like to bring you _____

_____

I Pledge to…

Give You Time

I want to give you some time. Maybe you need time to cuddle and not feel guilty about the chores, so I will do your laundry. Maybe you need some time to yourself, so I will come hold the baby while you shower and nap. Maybe you need to go out shopping or have someone run an errand for you. I will check in with you and coordinate a time for me to help. I just want to take care of you, whether you need me in the first few weeks or down the road.

Name: _____

I would be happy to _____

_____

Name: _____

I would be happy to _____

_____

Name: _____

I would be happy to _____

_____

Name: _____

I would be happy to _____

_____

Name: _____

I would be happy to _____

_____

Name: _____

I would be happy to _____

_____

Name: _____

I would be happy to _____

_____

Name: _____

I would be happy to _____

_____

Name: _____

I would be happy to _____

_____

Name: _____

I would be happy to _____

_____

I Pledge to…

Be Supportive

I want to be there for you when you are in need. I hope this journal helps you, but nothing can replace having a real conversation. Please call or text me if you ever want someone to talk to, even if it's just to have interaction with an adult! I promise to listen, I promise not to judge. I will also try to check in with you and let you know that I'm thinking of you. I just want to take care of you, whether you need me in the first few weeks or down the road.

Name: _____

Phone or Email: _____

Name: _____

Phone or Email: _____

Name: _____

Phone or Email: _____

Name: _____

Phone or Email: _____

Name: _____

Phone or Email: _____

Name: _____

Phone or Email: _____

Name: _____

Phone or Email: _____

Name: _____

Phone or Email: _____

Name: _____

Phone or Email: _____

Name: _____

Phone or Email: _____

Name: _____

Phone or Email: _____

A Note from the Author

I hope you find this journal relatable and helpful during your journey into motherhood. I tried to present a lot of common issues that a lot of mothers might face, but as every situation is unique, I'm certain that there are areas that I've missed. Regardless, even if these topics are those that best represent your experience, I don't expect that my words or anyone else's will necessarily give you all the answers to each trouble. Instead, I hope you take away a feeling—a feeling that you are not alone in this, that people care about you, and that you'll come out of trying times all the better for it.

Besides possibly missing out on some more specific or perhaps less common topics, you might notice that I also speak in a lot of generalities. I do this because this journal is yours and yours alone. I don't know you, so I'm not going to pretend I know what you need to hear. There are a lot of different parenting books and types of parenting styles out there; that's not what this book it about. I hope *Mommy Motivators* helps each mom find strength and trust in herself and her relationships with those who help complete her book. You will figure out what works best for you and your family.

If you'd like to hear more from me though, or get more information on motherhood topics, please visit my website at:

www.mommotivators.com

Acknowledgments

I thank all who in one way or another contributed in helping me see this project to fruition.

I greatly appreciate the significant labor taken by Paul Kvederis and Jennifer Hoffman to read and edit my drafts. You certainly taught me a thing or two along the way. Any remaining errors are entirely my own. Your encouragement and suggestions helped me to take this project farther than I ever imagined.

Thank you to others who took the time to read this book and provide their insight, including Shelley Katsuki, Tiffany Hutcheson, Leah Ribblett, Brett Engler, and Rachel Smith. I also appreciate the initial brain-storming session with Christopher Frace that helped boost my confidence!

Of course, I am forever grateful to my parents for all the love and support they have given me. Thank you also for listening to my idea especially in its early stages and for providing your feedback and encouragement.

To my husband, thank you for believing in me. You boost my creativity, listen to all my ideas, and share in all my excitement of this project.

Above all, thank you God, for hearing my prayers.

Made in the USA
Monee, IL
10 February 2020

21559532R00079